A Midsummer Night's Dream In Stratford:
A Very Long Poem

Martin Avery

A Midsummer Night's Dream In Stratford
ISBN #978-1-312-38051-6
Copyright C Martin Avery, 2014

Dedication: To Cynthia Langill, the actress turning into an author.

Audience Advisory: In general, we recommend this production for ages 8 and up, though it does contain occasional elements of sexual humour that some parents may consider unsuitable. The staging employs haze, smoke, ultraviolet light and simulated laser effects. (From the Stratford Festival website for A Midsummer Night's Dream, 2014.)

A Midsummer Night's Dream In Stratford:
A Very Long Poem

Martin Avery

A Stratford Romance

I lost a novel I wrote a decade or so ago
called A Stratford Romance, all about a
romantic summer in Stratford, and
that happens, sometimes, if you
write a lot of books, so you don't even
remember writing some of them,
which sounds unlikely or even
impossible if you've never
written a book or only written one
or two and I don't remember many of
the details about A Stratford Romance
except for one scene that takes place
on the Festival Theatre Stage at the end of
A Midsummer Night's Dream, and this
sounds like fiction but I swear it
really happened one summer
I spent in Stratford, taking a Drama course,
with a great group of teachers, and we saw
all the productions at Stratford that summer
including The Tempest, Dracula.
A Midsummer Night's Dream
Pride and Prejudice, The Alchemist
The School for Scandal, West Side Story
Macbeth, Glenn, Richard II, and we all
went to see Dream together, so we all
saw the same thing: a lot of slapstick with
the four young lovers played by
Melinda Deines as Hermia, Michelle Giroux as
Helena, Graham Abbey as Lysander and Martin
Albert as Demetrius with Jordan Pettle as
Nick Bottom and Brian Bedford as Puck

plus Seana McKenna as Titania,
Juan Chioran as Oberon, Diane D'Aquila as
Hippolyta, and some fairies, and, more
importantly, we watched when a doctor
got called out of the audience, from his
seat in the front row, and how his date
got called onto the stage, after the play was
over, and she refused to go, at first, but
eventually got talked into it, and when she
got up there, they showed her one of the
special effects, re-creating the moment when
rose petals fall from the sky, or the ceiling,
and just then her date re-appeared, entering
the stage from back-stage, carrying a
cushion, which he tossed on the ground
and then kneeled on, with one knee, as he
got down on one knee to propose to her,
holding up an engagement ring, and
everybody sighed as it was such a
romantic gesture but then gasped because
instead of accepting and giving the guy
a great big kiss his girlfriend slapped his
face and stomped off! And the gossip
we heard the next day was that she was
angry, humiliated, disappointed, ticked
off, because she was a very private person
and believed her engagement should be a
private event, not a showcase with a big
audience, and she decided that the guy
did not know her, if he thought she would
like all that attention, so she decided
marriage to him would be some kind of
over-produced nightmare she would never
like, so she broke it off and took off and

the most romantic proposal we had ever
witnessed turned out to be a complete
bust, a bomb, a performance that got
a very bad review!

I remember that production of Midsummer
as a very romantic retelling of the
well-known story and I remember that
summer as a very romantic time and
I remember that drama course as one of
the best educational experiences and
I have often wondered about that
proposal on the stage after A Midsummer
Night's Dream, how that guy arranged
it all, faking a call for an emergency, so
he got called out of the performance,
the only time I've ever seen that
at Stratford, and how he arranged to
have some of the cast remain on stage
after a standing ovation and curtain calls
and how he got some of the crew to
cooperate as well so they got his
girlfriend to go on stage and showered her
with rose petals, and how it was that he was
so romantic and so wrong, how it was that
he wanted her so much, wanted to marry her
so bad, and how he misjudged the whole
situation so completely. It was a moment
I haven't forgotten, it was so
Shakespearean, such a combination of
romance, comedy, and tragedy, with a body
left bleeding on the stage at the end of the
performance piece.

About Midsummer

Threatened with death if she marries against
her father's wishes, Hermia elopes with her lover,
Lysander, pursued by rival suitor Demetrius and
his spurned admirer, Helena. In the enchanted woods,
love's lunacy reaches its giddiest heights – both for
the bewildered couples and for an aspiring
actor transformed into the unlikely consort of
a fairy queen.

The reviews for the 2014 production of A
Midsummer Night's Dream in Stratford were
pretty impressive, mostly ....

"wonderfully creative" - Sun Media
"hysterical" - Sun Media
"sheer joy" - Sun Media
"palpable sizzle" - The Globe and Mail
"This is a Dream to beguile everyone,
from preteens to the most jaded theatregoers." - The Grid
"... the perfect family celebration of diversity"- The Grid
"****" (out of four) - Detroit Free Press
"among the funniest I have ever seen" - Detroit Free Press
"I can't recall ever seeing a production in which the audience and the actors were having a
better time" - Detroit Free Press
"Shakespeare would approve" - Detroit Free Press

However, the Toronto Star's review of
the play was not good. Here's what the
Star had to say, in the form of a poem,
let's call it a found poem, found in the
Toronto Star, or on their website, at
www.thestar.com/entertainment/stage/

2014/06/01/a_midsummer_nights_dream
A Midsummer Night's Dream: Review
By: Richard Ouzounian Theatre Critic,
Published on Sun Jun 01 2014
A Midsummer Night's Dream
.5 star
By William Shakespeare. Directed by Chris Abraham.
STRATFORD—During the previews of
Chris Abraham's production of
A Midsummer Night's Dream, the word on the street was
that it was a show people would either love or hate.
It opened at the Festival Theatre on Saturday night and
I was there.
Count me among the haters.
Let me make it clear that my dislike of the show
had nothing to do with its central framing device
(that it's all being performed to celebrate the marriage of
two men) or its selective use of gender-blind casting
(Titania is played by a man, Lysander by a woman).
No, what bothered me so profoundly was that it's
the kind of show that will sacrifice any sort of logic for
a cheap laugh and that most of the yocks generated during
the evening come from extraneous business
and cheap anachronistic ad libs, almost never from
the words of William Shakespeare.
Would you like some examples?
If we are indeed in 2014 and are supposed to believe
Hermia and Lysander as a lesbian couple who are
running off together, why would Hermia suddenly
play all coy when they bed down for the night and
hide inside an inflatable tent, which then proceeds to lurch
"humourously" all over the place as
Lysander unsuccessfully puts the moves on her.
And if Lysander then goes to sleep totally wrapped up in

a sleeping bag with no clothes showing, how does
Puck know to sprinkle the love-inducing herb on
her because "Weeds of Athens he doth wear"?
In a later scene, when the same poor lovers suddenly discover
a table full of wedding cake and cupcakes at centre stage
(meant for the wedding celebration), why
do these characters in a play start using the desserts from
the evening's "reality" to generate a massive food fight?
Those are just a few of dozens of examples I could have given.
Director Abraham only cares about how many in-jokes and
wannabe-hipster-meta laughs he can get by mocking the text.
The only person who actually gets away with it is
Mike Shara's Demetrius, who is the frat boy of your nightmares,
but plays it with such dedication and swaggering charm that
you somehow forgive him.
As for the other lovers, Bethany Jillard's Hermia is fine when
she's not whining, Liisa Repo-Martell as Helena seems to have
lost all the subtlety and variety she displayed in King Lear and
Tara Rosling initially makes a fine and sexy Lysander until
she is forced into horrible overdrive by Abraham.
For the rest? Well, Scott Wentworth dispenses his usual
ease on stage and grace with blank verse as Theseus, but
Maev Beaty delivers the first embarrassing performance
I've ever seen out of her as Hippolyta, because
Abraham makes her spend the whole final scene getting
Lindsay Lohan drunk.
As the other "regal" couple, Jonathan Goad has
a nice swagger as Oberon and delivers the poetry with
real edge, but he eventually gets defeated by
the silliness. (There's a pool of water on stage that
it seems everyone has to get drenched in eventually, like
Abraham was running a wet t-shirt contest for the entire cast.)
Evan Buliung as his consort, Titania makes, well, a very
solid woman, but he does a really nice job with his line in

sassy ad libs, even if some of them eventually undercut
the sincerity of Oberon's reconciliation with him.
(For the record, Goad and Buliung alternate the roles,
but I don't think that flip-flop would substantially change the show.)
There are far too many cute kids playing fairies and also
supposedly being adorable singing pop songs, as if
Stratford needed to find another Justin Bieber.
And as the leader of all the fairies, Chick Reid plays
Puck as Judge Judy.
That surely is not the way to do it.
Do those lovable comic characters the rustic mechanicals save
the day? Alas, no.
Stephen Ouimette starts out funny with a conception of Bottom as
a greasy pseudo-macho barbecue king, but
it eventually degenerates into a blandly generic performance.
And the rest of his cohorts have nothing to do with
the rest of the style of the play, with
a final sure-fire comedy scene that
misfires totally for the first time in my memory.
This production has nothing to do with
gender equality, shifting sexual roles or
anything of any real significance.
It's Value Village Shakespeare, a total surprise
coming from Abraham after last year's excellent Othello.
Let's hope this is just an aberration, the kind
that can happen to even a talented director on
a midsummer night.

That's the end of that review.
And what can we say?
Ouch!
My review would not go that way!
Neither did the review in
The Globe And Mail.
Let's give the Globe review
equal time and the same

treatment: This is a found poem,
found in The Globe And Mail online.

A Midsummer Night's Dream:
Stratford gloriously uplifts
overdone Shakespeare comedy
J. Kelly Nestruck
Stratford, Ont. — The Globe and Mail
Published Monday, Jun. 02 2014, 4:20 PM EDT
    Title A Midsummer Night's Dream
    Written by William Shakespeare
    Directed by Chris Abraham
    Starring Stephen Ouimette, Evan Buliung
    Company Stratford Festival

Get into your car, get out to this Dream. Or,
if you live farther than driving distance from
Stratford, Ont., maybe get into a plane or onto a train.
Forgive the bastardized Billy Ocean. I'm just
trying to get into the topsy-turvy, 1980s synth-pop vibe that
animates director Chris Abraham's gloriously uplifting and
revivifying production of
the most overdone of Shakespeare's comedies.
I thought I could live without ever seeing another
A Midsummer Night's Dream.
But how can you not love a version that features
the comic genius Stephen Ouimette as Bottom
barbecuing in a "Daddio of the Patio" apron
at the beginning, then singing New Order's
Bizarre Love Triangle amid a raging dance party at the end?
(Consider that a warning, too: If you can't, then you won't.)

Bottom, of course, is the weaver and amateur actor transformed
into a donkey who stars in the play-within-a-play that concludes
A Midsummer Night's Dream. His awful production of
Pyramus and Thisbe is presented as a gift at the nuptials of
Athenian rulers Theseus and Hippolyta, as well as
those of the play's quartet of lovers, finally and properly matched.

In Abraham's vision of the show, however, the entirety of
Dream is presented as a wedding gift – to two young men

getting married in a Stratford, Ont., backyard. Thus,
this Dream is presented with a host of young children
(who play the fairies, not just cutely, but astutely, and
never fail to bring a smile to your face) in the cast, an
onstage wedding DJ providing synth underscoring and
sound effects throughout, and the cream of the crop of
Stratford's acting company essaying unexpected roles and
treating the show and their parts with the irreverent joy and
anachronistic fun that you might in such a situation.

In a play that is about love and transformation,
Abraham has, fittingly, made a few changes to the characters.
At the start of the play, Hermia (Bethany Jillard) wants to
marry Lysander (Tara Rosling), but
her father Egeus wants her to marry Demetrius
(preening Mike Shara);
on the outside looking in is Helena (Liisa Repo-Martell),
who wants her ex Demetrius back.
The twist here is that Lysander is played as a woman by
a woman – and Rosling displays great nobility pleading her
love in the role at the start. "I am beloved of beauteous Hermia:
Why should not I then prosecute my right?"
she says movingly, and with same-sex rights denied in
so much of the world still, this acquires a
powerful resonance that it usually does not
(but which is probably roughly equivalent to
the resonance the original situation had in Shakespeare's time).

The other major shift is that Jonathan Goad and Evan Buliung play
the monarchs of the fairy world, Oberon and Titania, and
alternate between the roles.
On opening night, Buliung was the Fairy Queen –
and, despite his cis-male status, he was the best
I have ever seen,
regal and eerily otherworldly
(and never for a moment like a panto dame).
He and Goad, who
takes great advantage of the production's concept to
ad lib and play to the audience, have a
palpable sizzle in a part of the play that really feels like
it takes place in another dimension.

(Thank composer/sound designer Thomas Ryder Payne,
who also plays the DJ, in part for this.)

Shakespeare at Stratford is not particularly known for
sexual chemistry – but Jillard and Rosling have it
in spades here too, especially in a cleverly staged and
very hot scene that takes place away from
the audience's eyes inside of a camping tent set up
on stage. Abraham allow endless opportunities for
well-executed physical comedy here –
Rosling pulls some fine Pepé le Pew moves when
Lysander is under the influence of Puck's love juice, while
Shara gets many of the best moments preening as
Demetrius, rotating slowly in Helena's imagination, or
throwing children-fairies across the stage in a fury.

The Mechanicals, which include Lally Cadeau as
an uptight Peter Quince, are not perhaps
the funniest I've seen – but, for once,
their scenes seem in balance with the rest of the play.
And, thanks to Abraham's framing of the evening,
I finally really understood why Shakespeare includes
their performance of the tragedy of Pyramus and Thisbe
at the end. These wise fools are showing
what happens when you erect ridiculous walls
(and Keith Dinicol is an especially ridiculous Wall here)
between love;
it's that world, the one of tragedy, that is foolish,
while the world Bottom describes –
where "reason and love keep little company together"
– is the happy and sensible one.

There are moments one could quibble with:
Chick Reid's Puck and Liisa Repo-Martell's Helena are
remarkably unremarkable in parts that are usually
fan favourites, while the whole quartet of lovers occasionally
blast their verse into oblivion amid the mayhem.
Abraham's production also ends in what seems like
an endless competition of epilogues between
Bottom, Oberon, Puck and Theseus –
and it's a shame that though Egeus is played as

deaf in the play,
a deaf actor wasn't hired for this rare opportunity
to play at Stratford.

But this is a production better to just love blindly.
"There's no sense in telling me the wisdom of the fool won't
set you free," sings Bottom, who, by the end of the play,
knows a thing or two about bizarre love triangles.
And, yes, beyond the laughs and a few joyful tears, there is
something about Abraham's Dream that makes you feel
as if you've been set free, particularly after
an opening week of solid, but stuffy versions of
classic plays at Stratford.

Follow J. Kelly Nestruck on Twitter: @nestruck
More Related to this Story
Crazy for You: Stellar choruses plus
thrilling choreography equals
an exhilarating musical

Shakespeare And Cleopatra

Before we saw the Stratford 2014 production
of A Midsummer Night's Dream, we
wandered through the Festival store across
from the Theatre to browse books and
recordings and tee-shirts and other souvenirs
of the Stratford Festival Theatre for the
summer and discovered funky dolls for
Cleopatra and Shakespeare sitting side by
side on matching tables against a wall so
I picked up one of each and made them
trade places so Shakespeare was surrounded
by Cleopatras and Cleo was surrounded by
Shakespeares and picked up a pair to show
Cyn who surprised me after I said that
a lot of people who do past life work say
they were somebody famous and a lot of
women claim they were Cleopatra but
only a few men say they were Shakespeare
and she said, That was us, but I was
Shakespeare and you were Cleopatra.
She has an odd way of talking, sometimes,
so it sounds she is quite certain about
some things, speaking with the voice of
authority, and it sounded as though she
knew in her bones that she was a man
in a previous lifetime and that man was
William Shakespeare and I was quite
surprised by that but even more surprised
the she was quite certain I was a famous
woman from Egypt who happens to be
someone I quote quite often, as I like to say,
"Endless variety," and claim it comes from
Cleopatra and I often think about past lives,
unlike Cyn, and past lives in Egypt, and
time travel using Egypt as a portal or
station and I've written about the pyramids
when they were covered with an
encyclopedia of information which
they say Jesus studied and I've dreamed

about having a past life in Alexandria or
Cairo or somewhere along the Nile that
looks like the Garden of Eden when
time travel was common and popular and
I was a time travel agent arranging trips
from one time and place to another and
2. Back At Balzac's For Breakfast Again

Cyn and I spent the morning, lunch, and
afternoon at Balzac's again, from around
11 in the morning, after breakfast at our
hotel, the St. Albert Inn, or their
restaurant, called Let Them Eat Cake,
until around 4 in the afternoon, over
five hours, drinking strong coffee and
writing like Balzac, surrounded by
Balzac posters, inhaling Balzac Blend
coffee, watching Fiona Reid walk in and
out again, like a character in
The Time Traveller's Wife and
Cyn was working on her book, her
memoir, her autobiography, called
God Shots, which I wanted her to call
Hollywood, Hell, And Home, while
I finished book one in this duology
and changed the title from
Breakfast With Balzac, Lunch With Fellini
to Crazy For Stratford, and published it
online through Lulu and then started
right in on book #2 of the two, which
doesn't have a title yet, maybe
I'll call the two books together
Breakfast With Balzac, Lunch With Fellini
or The Yin And Yang Of Stratford or
maybe another title will pop into my head
as I write this long poem.

How I love long poems, now; they are
new to me but as old as literature, older
than Shakespeare, and perfect for me at
this stage as they all for all the freedom of

freefall or free-writing in free verse which
allows me to go at the speed I feel like
writing these days which is one hundred
miles per hour as I am jacked up on
Balzac's cafe mocha and Cyn likes to
see me speeding on Red Bull and
I've spent the last year in China getting
Traditional Chinese Medicine including
fire cupping with tu-nai or finger needling
with acupuncture including warm needles
and don't forget moxibustion and herbal
patches as well as tea and a formula to
drink so my chi or energy is flowing like
never before or not since I was a
young punk, a long time ago, now, but
it doesn't feel like it, and I'm writing
faster and better than ever, I believe, after
writing 100 books in The West and then
moving to The East to write 100 more, and
it took me decades to write the first thirty
and under a year to write the last thirty so
here we go with #140 (or so).

Our Review Of Midsummer Night

We really liked the 2014 production of
A Midsummer Night's Dream in
Stratford from the moment we walked in
to the moment we walked out. While we
waited for the play to start, we watched
the seats fill up with audience members and
we noticed that they all looked older than
us, with a few exceptions, and they all looked
as though they had spent their whole lives
reading books and watching plays, or
movies, not jogging or swimming, so
they looked like intellectuals, not athletes.
What did you expect? Cyn said. This is a
theatre, not a gym. We liked
the Festival Theatre stage, decorated to
look like a back yard in Muskoka, we
decided, with a lot of green, including
grass and trees, with a little pond, plus
patio lanterns, and it reminded me of
Cyn's back yard. If only it had a guy
practicing guitar on the back door steps,
I said, because her big brother used to
do that all the time, and then a guy
came out to play guitar, and then
the play started with two guys kissing
at centre stage, a white man and a
black man, and we knew we were in for
a night of theatre that would challenge
contemporary ideas about relationships
in a way Shakespeare would not have
done it but in a way that might be on the
same level as the way he did it back in
his day. I'd rather see a traditional or
classic production of this play, Cyn said,
at the interval, or half-time, when we
went for a walk, to stretch our legs,
and kept on walking, all the way back
to our little hotel, just ten blocks or so
away from the theatre, and we felt a

little bad about missing the second half
but the reviews suggested it turned into
a wet tee-shirt contest and we were
a little tired after seeing three plays in
three days with one more the next day
so we didn't feel too bad about missing
half of Midsummer, even though we
missed half of King Lear, the day before,
and it was a much more traditional
production, more like Shakespeare
would have done it, although the
emphasis was not on the plot, it was on
the star, it was all about King Lear, as
an aging ruler suffering from dementia
and we both had people close to us who
were suffering from dementia, so,
you know how it goes, sometimes,
when a play or movie strikes a little too
close to home and you can appreciate
the artistry and even benefit from the
catharsis of seeing a situation that's
important to you on the stage with
great actors but it's just not what you
want to see at the moment, and so
we did not stay for the second half of
either of the Shakespearean productions
at Stratford in the summer of 2014 and
that's not meant as a judgement on the
plays or actors or any aspect of the
experience, it was just what we wanted
to do at the time, and we felt free to
do what we wanted to do, and we were
happy we did it, despite the fact we
wanted to experience and celebrate
everything the Stratford Festival
had to offer. It was like skipping dessert
after a fantastic meal: we didn't
need it or want it even though we
recognized the fact that it would
be terrific.

Prolific Authors

Good news and bad news tonight
from around the world and
right here at home. First of all,
a Malaysian Airlines plane was
shot down over Ukraine and
hundreds died.
A Boeing 777 passenger plane of
the Malaysia Airlines crashed in
eastern Ukraine en route from
Amsterdam to Kuala Lumpur with
all 295 people on board feared dead.
The Ukrainian government and
rebels in the region accused each other
of shooting down the plane.
Secondly, wildfires out west in Canada are
the biggest in history, apparently,
and are threatening the town of
Banff as well as polluting the
skies of Edmonton.

Here in Stratford, my car got
stickered for being parked in the wrong
place. And then I Googled the
list of the world's most
prolific authors and discovered
I do not have a shot at the
record. The good news is that
I might be able to break into
the top twenty. The other news is
that I no longer care, because of
the other news from Malaysia
and Ukraine and Western Canada.

In case you care, here's the list
of the most prolific authors in
the history of the planet:

1. MARY FAULKNER (1903-1973) 904 books
South African writer Mrs. Mary Faulkner, whom

the Guinness Book of World Records ranks as
history's most prolific novelist, wrote under
six pen names and her novels include
There Is No Yesterday, Wind of Desire, and Harvest of Deceit.

2. LAURAN PAINE (b. 1916) 850 + books
American paperback novelist using 70 pen names.
Paine wrote a lot of westerns, such as
The Man from Wells Fargo (1961).

3. PRENTISS INGRAHAM (1843-1904) 600 + books
American dime novelist who occasionally wrote a
35,000-word book overnight. He wrote 200 books on Buffalo Bill alone.

9. GEORGES SIMENON (b. 1903) 500 + books
Belgian-born mystery writer with more than 200 books
published under his own name and over 300 published
under 17 pen names. His most famous character is Inspector Maigret.

11. EDWARD L. STRATEMEYER (1862-1930) 400 + books
American founder of the publishing syndicate that put out
the Nancy Drew and Hardy Boys and other popular children's series.

19. ALEXANDRE DUMAS pere (1802-1870) 277 books
The famous French author of The Three Musketeers and
The Count of Monte Cristo said to Napoleon III that he had
written 1,200 volumes, but that, of course, was in the days of
multivolume novels. (Musketeers originally filled eight volumes.)
His complete works were collected in 277 volumes,
most of which he wrote with collaborators.

20. L. T. MEADE (1854-1914) 258 books

It was a strange day for Cyn and I as we
wrote for over five hours in Balzac's and then
we were cranky so we went our
separate ways for the rest of the afternoon and
the early evening but got together again for
A Midsummer's Night Dream at the
Stratford Festival Theatre and we liked the
production but left at the interval because

we were tired and then I discovered
my car got stickered and the world news was
depressing, the national news was worse, and
the most prolific writers in the history of
literature have written ten times as many
books as me.

Cyn and I decided to call it a night early
but I stayed up to 11 surfing the net and
working on this book, but then I
hit the sack, hoping to
meditate my way to sleep while
remembering to work on
enlightenment so the evening would end
on a higher note and the next day would be
better than this one.

Southern Ontario Gothic

Friday morning, after an unsettled day,
I got up early to feed the meter, make sure
the car was okay, and decided to keep our
rooms for another day, so we would be
free to come and go as we pleased.
Cyn slept in so I had the breakfast special at
Let Them Eat Cake by the Albert Street Inn
on my own, feeling lonely, missing my
old life in China, feeling reverse
culture shock after seventeen days in my
home and native land.
I have bags under my eyes the likes of which
I've never had before and I feel a little tired,
which is odd, for me, so maybe international
travel does not agree with me. I've never
been a jet-setter so traveling half way around
the world and back is new to me and maybe
it's tiring me out. I'm saying "maybe"
a lot and I guess that means I'm not feeling
certain about .... anything.
Is that part of culture shock, or reverse
culture shock? What is it I miss about
China, or Asia, or is it just Dalian, my
little corner of the big continent and
the crowded country, the city of
six million called the Paris of China.
I've been writing about Balzac and
feeling his presence a great deal and
Balzac wrote about Paris and now
I live in the Paris of China and
think of myself as the Balzac of
China, in a way, as well as the
Balzac of Canada. Oy veh! That's not
the way I think of myself at all!
I'm just a guy who writes a lot and
teaches high school and likes
books and theatre and nature and
worries about the planet's politics
and environment. I feel worried

this morning, which is not usual
for me. Maybe I need more sleep.
Maybe I need more love. Maybe
I miss the excitement of my
life in China and all the love
I felt while I was there. I miss
seeing so many Asian faces,
being the only white face in
a big crowd, feel funny sitting in
the audience of the Stratford Festival
theatre surrounded by white people
who are not thin and look as though
they have spent their lives
sitting around reading books and
watching plays and movies and
not running around trying to
survive the way the people of
Dalian have for the past
half century, or longer. I thought
Canadians were a long stronger.
Maybe the white faces I see
around me belong to Americans
who have crossed the border,
leaving the U.S.A. for Canada
in the summer, to see
Shakespeare in Stratford.
Maybe, maybe, maybe.

I woke up thinking about
Timothy Findlay: Timothy Irving
Frederick Findley, OC, O.Ont.,
a Canadian novelist and playwright,
informally known by the nickname
Tiff or Tiffy, an acronym of his initials.
I saw his star on the sidewalk by the
Avon Theatre while I was walking
yesterday, looking for Red Bull and
Preparation H. -- Too much information?
I was looking for energy and for
something to take away the
bags under my eyes so I

looked energized and felt
like going to the theatre to see
A Midsummer Night's Dream.

Tiff? Cyn said. Who's that?
She loves Canada but has never
been a huge fan of CanLit
until now. Timothy Findlay
was part of the original
Stratford Festival company in
the 1950s, acting alongside
Alec Guinness, and also played in
Sunshine Sketches,
the CBC Television adaptation of
Stephen Leacock's Sunshine Sketches
of a Little Town.

Findley declared his homosexuality as
a teenager, but married actress/photographer
Janet Reid for a couple of years and
eventually became the domestic partner of
writer Bill Whitehead. They collaborated on
several documentary projects in the 1970s,
including the television miniseries
The National Dream and Dieppe 1942.

Findley's first two novels,
The Last of the Crazy People (1967) and
The Butterfly Plague (1969), were
published in Britain and the United States
after having been rejected by Canadian publishers.
Findley's third novel, The Wars, was
published to great acclaim and went on to win
the Governor General's Award for fiction and
was adapted for film in the 1980s.

Timothy Findley was a founding member
and chair of the Writers' Union of Canada
and a president of the Canadian chapter of
PEN International. His writing was typical of
the Southern Ontario Gothic style —

Findley, in fact, first invented its name —
and was heavily influenced by Jungian psychology.
Mental illness, gender and sexuality were
recurring themes in his work. His characters
carried dark personal secrets, and were
conflicted — sometimes to the point of psychosis.

Findley and Whitehead resided at
Stone Orchard, a farm near Cannington,
Ontario, and in the south of France, and
Findley was honoured by the French,
who declared him a
Chevalier de l'Ordre des arts et des lettres.

Findley was the author of dramas for
television and stage. Elizabeth Rex,
his most successful play, premiered at
the Stratford Festival of Canada to
rave reviews and won him another
Governor General's award.

 In the final years of Findley's life,
declining health led him to move
his Canadian residence to
Stratford, Ontario, and he in 2002, in
Brignoles, France, not far from
his place in Cotignac.

He would have loved Stratford's
2014 production of Midsummer
Night's Dream, I think. I saw his
play here in Stratford, Elizabeth
Rex, and I've read his novels, and
taught The Wars several times.

I feel close to Tiff this morning,
here in Stratford, like a strange
character in a novel in the sytle
of Southern Ontario Gothic.

Cottage Gothic

My first book was called Cottage Gothic
and book stores often placed it in the
architecture or building section of their
stores as the term gothic refers to
architecture and cottage gothic is the
term used to describe

What is Gothic literature?
That which we classify as "Gothic" is a subgenre of
the Romantic movement of the 19th century
starting with Horace Walpole's novel
The Castle of Otranto. -- I like that name,
Otranto .... Sounds like a mash-up of
Ontario and Toronto .... Maybe I'll use it ....

Originally, what we call "Gothic" in terms of architecture
was called the modern or French style by its contemporaries
and Gothic architecture was all about the introduction of
light and height to the churches through the use of
flying buttresses, pointed arches, ribbed vaulting and
stained glass windows. The idea was for the church to
become a medium between Earth and Heaven through
its height and the heavenly light.

Gothic Cottage may refer to Carpenter Gothic,
the architectural style, or Rural Gothic, a
North American architectural style using
wood for details that were carved in stone
in authentic Gothic architecture, characterized by
its profusion of jig-sawn details, after
the invention of the steam-powered scroll saw
often using board and batten siding.

"American Gothic" is a painting by
Grant Wood from 193o inspired by
a cottage designed in the Carpenter Gothic
style with a distinctive upper window and
a decision to paint the house along with
"the kind of people I fancied should live in that house."

So... what is Gothic literature?
Gothic is a genre that incorporates themes of
eternal conflict and importance to
the human condition - relationships, gender,
patriarchy, nostalgia, and the sublime.
It looks away from the present to the past and
from what is obvious and scientific towards
an inner world that is at once liberating and
imprisoning, and forces the reader to
engage it on its own terms, and not those of
social and cultural conditioning.

For Southern Ontario Gothic, think of
Timothy Findlay and Margaret Atwood and
Alice Munro, who won the Nobel Prize in
Literature, and for Central Ontario Gothic,
which is a little different, think of
Susan Swan and Mel Malton and me, and
for Canadian Gothic, think of Bear by
Marian Engel. -- I've met all these writers
and got to know some of them and I've
worked with others and feel
related to all of them.

When I was in grad school in the U.S.A.,
working with writers from all over America,
it did not surprise me that I hit it off with
Wally Lamb, who had a background
something like mine, but I was shocked
to discover I had a great deal in common
with a group of women writers from the
American South, but then I realized they
were writing American Gothic, or
American South Gothic, and we were all
writing about repression and the longing
for liberation, setting our stories in
moody places, like the Ontario described by
Susanna Moodie in Roughing It In The
Bush and "Life in the Backwoods, A Sequel to
Roughing it in the Bush" and Life in

the Clearings Versus the Bush.
-- Makes me think of my old hometown in
Muskoka called Gravenhurst which means
a graven clearing in a forest, the setting of
around half of my first 100 books.

P.S. I just Googled myself, looking for
Cottage Gothic, and discovered my
first book is now available for free along with
an audio book version, apparently, at
http://bookdir.info/?p=114934, with
a couple of great reviews.

Alice Through the Looking-Glass

By Lewis Carroll
Adapted for the stage by James Reaney
Directed by Jillian Keiley
Approximate running time:
2 hrs 12 min, including one interval

About the Play
Climbing through her living-room mirror,
Alice enters a world of wonders populated by
such fantastical characters as Humpty Dumpty,
Tweedledee and Tweedledum, the Walrus and
the Carpenter – and the fearsome Jabberwock.
Children and adults alike will be delighted by
this spectacular journey into the topsy-turvy
realm of the dreaming mind.

"visual and choreographic feast" - Toronto Star
"kaleidoscope of visual delight for kids of all ages"
"ideal for the whole family" - The Record
"childhood imagination reigns supreme"
"magical" - "great fun" - Sun Media

Audience Advisory
Recommended for ages 6 and up,
this production uses pyrotechnics.

Alice Through the Looking-Glass: Review
A visual and choreographic feast,
Alice Through the Looking-Glass really is
one show that's for kids of all ages.
By: Richard Ouzounian Theatre Critic,
Published on Sat May 31 2014
Alice Through the Looking-Glass

By James Reaney. Directed by
Jillian Keiley at the Avon Theatre.
Call it Cirque du Stratford.
The production of Alice Through the

Looking-Glass at the Avon Theatre
is so filled with visual velocity and
choreographic charm that our
show business cousins up in Quebec
had better look to their laurels.
Either that, or ask Jillian Keiley to
direct and Bretta Gerecke to design
their next production, as they have
done so splendidly with this one.

Let's be honest, the "Family Entertainment" slot
that Stratford has been hawking for some time now
is fraught with terrors. Some shows that
charm the real youngsters bore the teens silly and
perplex the parents, while others
that mom and dad enjoy find
brother and sister swatting each other with
programs before intermission.

But now for something completely different, as
Monty Python would say, and in fact, this totally
bizarre version of Alice Through the Looking-Glass is
like the child that the iconic British comedy troupe
might have conceived if they'd spent a wild night with
Guy Laliberté and his merry Québécois pranksters.

The script is by the late and venerable James Reaney,
based on Lewis Carroll's oft-adapted story of
what happens when a girl named Alice goes through a
looking-glass, down a rabbit hole, or
any combination of the above.

At first, this version starts straight and a bit slowly, but
once Trish Lindström's Alice (slightly off-centre with
a welcome touch of Amy Poehler about her) goes through
the mirror, it's anything goes and the devil take the hindmost.

At times, every member of the large cast, young and old,
male and female are all dressed like photographic negatives of
Alice: dark hair while hers is blond, wearing
blue pinafores dotted with white, whereas

Alice wears white dotted with blue.

That's simple to say, less simple to see, especially
when the drag acts include Tom McCamus,
Sanjay Talwar and Brian Tree, all of whom
make very odd young women indeed.

Then there's the younger men, like
Tyrone Savage or Gareth Potter, who
hold on to their handsome masculinity and
let it shine through the feminine disguise.
It's all strangely provocative.
But most of the time, it's just fun.
And it's spectacular fun as the cast members use
roller skates to move giant metal "trees" covered with
a variety of spectacular objects to take us into
that place truly known as Wonderland.
Just like a golden oldies radio program,
the hits keep a-comin', and I am loath to
give away too many of the surprises that include
cascading jelly beans, confetti cannons and
gigantic foam letters that spell, of course, A-L-I-C-E.
Yes, it's a non-stop riot, thanks to
Keiley's staging (assisted by Dayna Tekatch's eclectic
choreography), but now and then we actually
pause to allow some of the familiar scenes from
Carroll's work to emerge, interpreted with
total panache by the company.
You will be totally entranced by
Cynthia Dale's archly regal Red Queen, sending up
sky-high all the glamour-pusses she's ever played at
Stratford, or Brian Tree's magnificently sour
Humpty Dumpty, sprinkling a fine mist of
malt-vinegar pessimism on the
fish-and-chips comedy of his character.
You won't be able to get enough of
the Tweedledum of Mike Nadajewski,
collapsing on stage repeatedly like a
narcoleptic rag doll, or his partner,
the Tweedledee of Sanjay Talwar, who keeps
running in circles like a dog chasing its tail,

both of them delivering the ooziest
North Country accents you've ever heard.
And mention must, must, must be made of
the one and only Tom McCamus, whose
March Hare has droopy eyes any
basset hound would envy and whose
narrator is briskly wheeled onto the stage in
an armchair for a parody of
Masterpiece Theatre to deliver the richest
version of "Jabberwocky" you've ever heard.
To be totally honest, not every one of the
characterizations works, but those lapses are
few and far between, and the beautiful thing about
Keiley's production is that it's like
Vancouver weather: if you don't like it, wait
five minutes and it will change.
You know that much-abused phrase: for
children of all ages? This smashing production of
Alice Through the Looking-Glass truly deserves it.

If you don't know a child, rent one for
the afternoon and go see this show.

Review: Well played, Stratford, well played.
Alice Through the Looking-Glass at the Avon Theatre
Alice Through the Looking-Glass, by Lewis Carroll
Adapted for the stage by James Reaney
Produced in association with Canada's National Arts Centre
Directed by Jillian Kelley
Choreographed by Dayna Tekatch
Designed by Bretta Gerecke

The Story: Alice, having been sent to
her room "until she learns better manners",
retreats into her imagination, which takes her
into the world of her looking-glass, where
everything happens backwards. As she
makes her way across a giant chessboard to
become a queen, she meets a wide range of
impossible characters doing impossible
things, until she begins to suspect she is in

a dream - but whose dream is it?

Talk about a testament to the craftsmanship of
the props and costumes departments at
the Stratford Festival.
An army of anti-Alices in blue-and-white dresses,
wheeling around on an armada of bicycles attached to
which are a forest of trees (onto which the leaves fall
up) and giant flowers - not to mention the
inevitable mess of Newtonian fluid that is
all that is left of Humpty Dumpty after
he takes his great fall off his great wall.
And let us not forget the mile high or wide
prop-wigs worn by the White and Red Queens that
look like they weigh about ten pounds each.
My neck hurts just thinking about it.

Well, it is a fantasy after all, things are bound to
look quite fantastic, and the story makes about as
much sense as adult rules do to the children
like Alice who are expected to follow them.
Director Jillian Kelley's concept for the
production is as clear as it is likely to get with
such a story, the actors are given free reign to
be as over-the-top as necessary, and
the show often breaks the fourth wall -
to great effect for an audience full of children.

In fact, since the Stratford Festival has
marketed this production of
Alice Through the Looking-Glass for children since
the very start, I thought it only fair to
let my review be written by those for whom it was intended.
So at intermission I asked Ellie, Isaac, Berkeley and Miles
if they were enjoying the show, and why.
Ellie (age 6), wearing a sparkly mask in
the true spirit of the show, answered with
an enthusiastic "Yes! I want to know
what will happen next!" and confessed
she did not like the fire (sparklers, actually),
"because" she explained quite awed,

"I had the funny feeling it was real.
But my favourite part was when she
[Alice] touched the mirror and it went
around and around - it was really cool!"

Miles (age 4) liked a different part.
"Yeah," he said, "I liked when the bikes came out,"
referencing the bikes that became trees,
flowers and other gigantic props, "but
I like it all." (Miles also got to pull a
giant rope in the second half of the show after
intermission which no doubt became
his personal highlight.
I won't spoil what the rope-pulling wrought,
but it was a delightfully sweet surprise.)

Isaac (age 5) had the same favourite character as
the rest - Alice (played by Trish Lindstrom). "But
I really liked when the Red Queen said,
"Goodbye!" and jumped off the stage!"
This was actress Cynthia Dale, literally
throwing herself into the part, which
the young audience definitely appreciated if
Isaac was any indication.
But Berkeley (age 5) felt quite differently.
When asked if she was enjoying the show, she
answered with a grave frown and shake of
the head. Oh dear. "Why not, Berkeley?" I asked.
"It's too confusing," she said, still grave, and
patted her cheek. Her grandmother Gretchen
explained, "she didn't understand the part about
the gnat, and it bothered her" referencing
the talking bug that is both an actor
behind Alice an invisible mite that
Alice keeps swatting at and eventually smites
(by accident). At this point
Berkeley was pulling out a recent purchase from
the gift shop and leafing through it -
a copy of Alice in Wonderland.
"Berkeley, do you think you'll enjoy
the book more than the play?" I asked.

"YES!" came the emphatic reply. Oh dear.

Ok, so we head into the second half of the play,
where the Lion and the Unicorn
(Tyrone Savage and Gareth Potter respectively) have a
boxing / karate / mixed-martial-arts battle, we meet
Humpty Dumpty on his great wall - played to
absolute perfection by Brian Tree with
assistance from two of the anti-Alice Army -
and where the White Knight (Rylan Wilkie)
vanquishes the Red Knight (John Kirkpatrick),
serenades Alice, Alice finally becomes
a queen and returns to her own home.
My personal highlights?
Sarah Orenstein as a delightful White Queen,
bouncing around with that mile-high wig, and
Brian Tree's Humpty Dumpty, incidentally
the only actor whose English accent didn't sound
put on because he is English, and the
blink-and-you'll-miss-it-for-adults-only
Last Supper tableau (cheeky, wot?)

But back to the critics who matter.
I tracked some of them down at shows' end.
Kaelynn (age 4) loved the Red Queen, and
when the White Knight sang to Alice
(a future musical theatre aficionado, methinks).
Her brother Kaine (age 5) loved
Tweedledee and Tweedledum
(Liverpudlian-sounding Sanjay Talwar and
Mike Nadajewski respectively) pulling Alice into
a game of Ring Around the Rosie, and
adamantly did NOT like "the part where
they put her [Alice] in her room." Understandably.

Clare (age 10) thought the whole thing "very cool.
The streamers and jellybeans were unexpected."
(Oh, spoiler alert!) Clare also felt that
Trish Lindstrom "captured a 7 and-a-half-year-old
exactly." Her mom Maureen loved
the cross-dressing Alices, which reminded her of

a Mark Morris ballet. "It just flips things
in your brain so you see things in a new way,"
she explained. "It challenges
preconceived ideas. I really enjoyed it."

And at this point Berkeley (age 5), our harshest
critic, came running up. "I really liked the second part!"
she burst out. "Humpty Dumpty was funny."
Her grandmother Gretchen chimed in.
"She perked up a lot with the jellybeans," she chuckled.

Well played, Stratford!

Alice Through the Looking-Glass
continues in repertory until October 12.
The forecast for each performance is bright,
with a brief shower of jellybeans.

Leaving Stratford

Such sweet sorrow, as Shakespeare said.
Leaving Stratford is always hard but
we have learned to choose how we
feel and so we are not sad it's over,
we are happy it happened, or maybe
we feel something more sophisticated
like soldage as we leave Stratford
thinking about how great it was and I
add this trip to Stratford to all my
other trips to Stratford to see Shakespeare
starting in high school and continuing
through university and then every year as
a high school teacher plus two summers as
a teacher taking drama courses and other
summer trips including last summer like
this summer and I remember the summer
I studied English and Drama in England
and flew back to Canada in time to catch
a play at Stratford just days after seeing
Shakespeare at the National Theatre in
London and you cannot compare two
great theatrical traditions on just two plays
but I have to say, at the risk of offending
everyone in England, that Canada's
Shakespeare was far superior, and now
that I've spent a year in China and have
a new perspective on Canada as well as
tourism and development and culture
I look at Stratford with new eye and
envision it developed even more so it's
an even greater attraction with a
beach nearby and a casino and twice
as many theatres and more Canadian
content and even more Shakespeare and
more big American musicals and maybe
no definitely a French theatre and an
Italian opera hall and a concert hall by
the casino and great places for theatre
from China, Japan, and everywhere.

And an airport and a high speed train.
And I can hardly wait to come back
to Stratford again.

Toronto Poetry

A lot of poetry has been written about Toronto
and at least one song has been written about
the highway called The 401, but writing poetry
about the highways around Toronto is
something that just isn't done. We write
Southern Ontario Gothic, about people with
profound problems, not highways or super
highways linking Toronto to Stratford or
Toronto to Hamilton, Niagara On The Lake,
Niagara Falls, London, Detroit, Western
Ontario, South Western Ontario, Paris,
Ontario, this green landscape of rolling
flatlands with the Niagara Escarpment in
and Rattlesnake Point in the centre of it
with Highway 401 cutting through it, a
black ribbon in the forest with fields of
corn and four lanes of bumper-to-bumper
traffic, all new cars, the latest models,
the top end, no longer just from the Big
Four auto-makers, but still some cars from
Detroit and Oakville, and more from
South Korea and Japan, and so many people
streaming in to Toronto from Stratford,
London, Hamilton, so you guess there must be
something special happening in the big city
on the weekend as usually the traffic is
heavy going the other way as the millions
of people who live in the city head out of
town on Friday night but this Friday night
millions of people were going to Toronto
to see the Blue Jays play a double-header
on the weekend, to see the big Indy car
race in Toronto, to see a Katy Perry concert,
and there was a Salsa Festival on St. Clair
Avenue, four big special events on top of
the city's many regular attractions, so
there we were, stopped on the 401, several
times, travelling at low speeds, speeding up
for short stretches, stopping, starting, seeing

the same cars again and again, watching
one jet after another fly overhead, flying
out of Pearson International, heading west
to Detroit, Chicago, Winnipeg, Vancouver,
Los Angeles, Australia, Japan, South Korea,
maybe even China, and in from the east,
bringing in more people from New York City
for the big weekend in Toronto and we
realized our usual route past Yorkdale
down the Allen Expressway to Eglinton
would be so crammed with cars it would
add another hour to a trip that was taking
twice as long as usual so we tried going
down Avenue Road and it appeared to be
clear so it felt as though we were witnessing
a miracle as we zipped down from the
jam-packed highway to The Eglinton Way
in seconds, maybe a few minutes, after
hours on The 401 but being forced to
go slow on a super-highway after a week in
Stratford to see the Shakespeare Festival
plus other plays is not such a bad thing as
you can see it as a metaphor about
what to do with the rest of your life or
a preview of life in Canada and in the
West and all over the world in the near
future, perhaps, or you can just be
happy that everybody had to slow down and
play it safe instead of flying down the
highway at 120 and noticing nothing about
the landscape of green fields and forest
with jet airplanes in the blue skies and
nobody shooting them down, unlike
what was happening in Russia or the
area Russia is fighting over, called Ukraine,
and the air is clear here, unlike China,
with its late industrial revolution fuelled by
coal, taking so many manufacturing jobs
out of southern Ontario and the U.S.A. as
everything is now made in China and now
China is looking for English teachers like

me as so many people there want to leave
that big crowded country for North America
to see our wilderness and experience the
freedom of democracy, which gave us
Rob Ford as the mayor of Toronto and
Stephen Harper as the prime minister of
Canada, or maybe they just want to
get rich doing business in the land of
capitalism and materialism and create
links between Asia and North America
and after a week in Stratford after
a year in China I am thinking it would be
a great business idea to copy Stratford and
re-create it in China as China has replicated
other places in the West so the Chinese
people don't have to travel to Paris or
England and Stratford, China, would be
a popular attraction anywhere in the big
country of 1.4 billion but especially in a
place like Dalian, where I live, as there is
no place like Dalian, with the Black
Mountains beside the Yellow Sea, the best
air in Asia, a short flight from Beijing,
Shanghei, Hong Kong, Tokyo, and Seol,
South Korea, if not North Korea, and
the part of the old Soviet Union we
knew as Siberia and as I drive the
Kia I rented from Stratford to Toronto
I'm relatively not unhappy about how
the history of the world has turned out
after the War in Korea, the Second
World War, the Cold War, the history of
China over the past century and the last
five thousand years, not to mention the
short history of Canada and the rich
history of the Western world which
has given us great literature celebrated
beautifully in Stratford, in southern
Ontario, halfway between Alice
Munro's hometown and the city where
Margaret Atwood lives, just south of

my old hometown which was the
birthplace of Norman Bethune and
1.4 billion Chinese people would love to
visit this place and some would like to
live here so it would be a great idea to
copy Stratford and also some other
parts of southern and central Ontario
as a Canadian and Western culture
theme park with more than four
theatres celebrating Shakespeare and
the literature of the world outside
China plus the literature and culture
of China and we could call it
Toronto, China, or Stratford, China,
or Southern Ontario, China, or,
for marketing purposes, Western
World, China. Now there's a concept
that would take millions to develop
or maybe billions but it would make
billions year after year for many years
to come as China develops fast with
its industrial revolution turning into a
consumer revolution that will change it
into a futuristic wonderland where
East meets West and combines the best
of both with what we have learned over
the past century and the last millennium
and the five thousand years of history
on this planet that we have treated like a
garbage dump but still looks so beautiful
in many places, especially Canada from
coast to coast to coast, as I noticed when
I flew over it, on Canada Day, and the
section called Southern Ontario, which
I drove through, slowly, in July of 2014
on my way from Stratford to Toronto
one summer in Canada on holiday, home
from China for a couple of months and
what better way to spend my time than
a trip to Stratford for a week of plays and
writing and with my friend from the old

days when we were the stars of our
Grade One class at the North Ward Public
School in Gravenhurst, just starting to
learn and teach English at the start of
our lives which would be so full of
culture with her acting in movies in
New York City and going to L.A. for
Hollywood movies and me writing
hundreds of books and the two of us
coming together again decades later to
write about it all and celebrate the best of
Western civilization on a road trip from
Toronto to Stratford and home in the
summer of 2014 while we tried to
forget about global warming and the
other warnings about impending
global disasters and enjoy the best of
the West while formulating a plan to
take it to the Far East and make big
bucks replicating Stratford in China
and making it even more of a cultural
theme park celebrating the best of
the East and the West.

The Great Wall Of China Books Series

1. From Bethune's Birthplace To The People's Republic Of China (memoir)
2. Swimming To China (poetry)
3. Mo Yan And Me (short novel)
4. Far Away, Dalian, Far Away (travel)
5. A Trip Around Lake Muskoka With Norman Bethune (short novel)
6. In Love And War
7. Chinese Kisses (poetry)
8. My Chinese Metamorphosis (poetry)
9. Hockey Night In China (non-fiction)
10. An Intro To Acupuncture And TCM (non-fiction)
11. Norman Bethune's Tears Cure Cancer (novel)
12. Bethune Returns To China (novel)
13. Bethune's Time (novel)
14. The Bethune Trilogy: A Trip Around Lake Muskoka With Norman Bethune, Bethune's Tears Cure Cancer, Bethune Returns To China
15. Good News From China (found poetry)
16. Suzanne Takes You Down (novel)
17. The Woman Who Was Picked Up By A Monk (poetry)
18. Bethune Buttons (poetry)
19. Dear China: Love Letter Poems
20. Dalian: A Long Poem (poetry)
21. The Way Of The Dragon (novel)
22. Past And Future Lives In China (fiction)
23. Love And Death In China (duology)
24. The Beijing-Vancouver Express: Connecting Toronto To Dalian, China to Canada
25. Dalian: A Long Poem
26. Toronto: A Long Poem
27. Toronto And Dalian: Two Long Poems
28. The Timeless Universal Etheric Library (poetry)
29. Oh Canada: A Long Poem On Canada Day
30. Holocaust Healing (novel)
31. My Chinese Enchantment (poetry)
32. Gravenhurst And China: A Long Poem

33. Crazy For Stratford: A Very Long Poem
34. A Midsummer Night's Dream In Stratford: A Very Long Poem
35. Stratford, China: A Long Poem

www.ingramcontent.com/pod-product-compliance
Lightning Source LLC
Chambersburg PA
CBHW021117020426
42331CB00004B/534